WHAT OTHERS ARE SAYING

My Life, My Care, My Way

"As a Clinical Education Consultant in the long-term care industry I travel nationwide and recognize the great need for this fantastic tool. A wealth of complex life choices can be captured in this easy to read/must do, for anyone who plans on getting old, but especially for those who don't plan!"

Danielle Bednarek VanHyfte, Clinical Education Consultant, healthcare trainer

"I look forward to completing my copy of "My Life, My Care, My Way." I see it as a valuable tool for those who may participate in my care."

Jerry Logue, retired educator

"I recently lost my grandmother who got sick and passed away in a matter of weeks. She had spent the past twenty-five years caring for my grandfather in their home. Fortunately, we knew my grandmother's wishes so we could spend our last days together simply enjoying each other. Not everyone can be taken care of by their spouse and many people might never share their wishes about their healthcare with their family. Paula's well thought out and compassionate workbook can help people document their own wishes for their own care so the time spent with family is meaningful, special and comfortable."

Dena J. Thorson, educator

"After reading through "My Life, My Care, My Way" my comment is that if ever I am in need of assistance in a nursing home or an assisted living environment, I hope and pray that caregiver is someone as caring and compassionate as Paula. I think the concept is excellent and think it would be a wonderful tool for family and care givers."

Susan Enns

"This approach invites persons to tell caregivers enough about themselves personally that care can be personal as well as professional. This is a helpful tool for both parties."

Pastor George C. O'Reilly

"The usefulness of this book to the elderly and terminally ill is priceless to them and their families. In the eight years I've worked in long-term care, I can't tell you how many times I've watched a family struggle to make decisions about a loved ones care without having the knowledge of what the person would have wanted. This book eliminates that problem and also gives the family a keepsake of the loved ones life. Thank you for allowing me to be a part of the process."

Wendy J. Vorderbruggen, RHIT

"I got so interested in the material! What a wonderful idea!"

Jon F. Burke, Ph. D

"Paula shared her experiences at our facility and obviously speaks from her heart. A lot of detail goes into this book and these details come from life experiences in caring for the elderly. The concept of this book makes one stop & think about our future as an older adult and the fact that this tool could actually help determine our quality of care in the ever changing world of healthcare. I feel this book would of course benefit our residents but it really got ME thinking. Paula has an impressive background in geriatric care and this stimulates interest and confidence in her endeavor. The Residents really enjoyed the presentation; they are still talking about it."

Kathleen A. Franklin, Activity Director, assisted living facility

"Everyone could benefit from the use of such a book. It is very useful, especially for the caregivers to help create a holistic plan of care"

Shilo N. Jackson, RN, health facility surveyor

"Paula has taken her knowledge about advanced care and her passion for helping others and created an amazing resource for our generation."

Kelley Eckler

"I love the concept. There is clearly a need for this type of communication between patients and caregivers."

Rebecca Bigelow, LVN/LPN

THIS BOOK HAS BEEN COMPLETED BY

_____

current photo
of yourself

My Life, My Care, My Way

My Advance Personal Care Plan

PAULA HARDER KENEMORE

Lake Effect Media

My Life, My Care, My Way

© 2007 by Paula Harder Kenemore

Published by:

Lake Effect Media
Post Office Box 452
Moose Lake, MN 55767-0452 U.S.A

Office: (218) 485-4252
Fax: (218) 485-4842

www.lakeeffectmedia.net
info@lakeeffectmedia.net

All rights reserved. No part of this book may be reproduced or transmitted in any form or by any means, electronic or mechanical, including photocopying, recording or by any information storage and retrieval system, without written permission from the author, except for the inclusion of brief quotations in a review.

This book is designed to provide accurate and authoritative information in regard to the subject matter covered. It is sold with the understanding that the publisher and author are not engaged in rendering legal, accounting, medical or other professional services. If you require legal, medical or other expert assistance, you should seek the services of a competent attorney or physician.

ISBN 978-0-9800579-6-6

Printed in the United States of America

Design by Dezime Graphics

DEDICATION

This book is dedicated to the memory of Terri Schiavo, who first inspired me to create a more complete tool for communicating healthcare wishes. To my husband Tom, my children, sisters and parents, may they always know what is in my heart, even if my heart no longer has a voice.

ACKNOWLEDGEMENTS

I would like to thank the very special people who participated in the making of this book. From designing, editing, critiquing, questioning, laughing, pushing, shoving, and encouraging, they put their own unique touch on this book: Debbie Zime, Danielle Bednarek VanHyfte, Becky Bigelow, Kathy Blasyck, Linda Bump, Jon Burke, Kelley Eckler, Jerry Enns, Sue Enns, Carol Flaming, Diane Harder, Paul Harder, Elijah Jackson, Shilo Jackson, Tom Kenemore, Jerry Logue, Pam Logue, Kimberly McGehee, Michael McGehee, George O'Reilly, Grant Stout, Dena Thorson, Wendy Vorderbruggen, Carol White, Philip White, and Diane Witt.

My Life, My Care, My Way

TABLE OF CONTENTS

Introduction 8
  Suggestions for Completing the Book 9

Personal Information 11
  Me & My Family 12
  Ethnic Background & Education 13
  Healthcare 14
  Politics & Religion & Spirituality 15
  Adaptive Equipment & Communication ...17
  My Ideal Life 19
  Thinking Ahead 19
  Additional Thoughts, Photos, Clippings ..20

Comforts 21
  How I Like to Present Myself 22
  Personal Appearance 23
  Daily Routine & Room Temperature 24
  Sleep Routine & Eating Habits 25
  Bathing & Volume Preferences 27
  Visual & Relaxation Preferences 28
  Exercise & Objects of Comfort 29
  Additional Thoughts, Photos & Clippings .30

Interests & Activities 31
  Interests & Activities 32
  Favorites 33
  Pets 34
  Accomplishments 35
  Social Circle 35
  Favorite Holidays & Traditions 38

Life History 39
  My Family 40
  Memories of Mother & Father 40
  Family Photos 41
  Memories of Spouse 42
  Photos of Spouse & Memories of Wedding ..43
  Photos of Children 44
  Memories of Children 45
  Memories of Grandchildren 46
  Photos of Grandchildren 47
  Memories of Siblings & Grandparents ...48
  Life Review 49
  Time of My Life 53
  Additional Thoughts, Photos, Clippings ..58

Personal Directives 59
  Legal & Financial Matters 60
  Legal Healthcare Directives 61
  Home Healthcare 61
  Assisted Living 62
  Nursing Home Care 63
  Medical Care 65
  Care for My Pet 68
  Spiritual Care 68
  End of Life Care 69
  Upon My Death 71
  My Funeral 72
  Special Requests 73
  A Personal Letter to My Family 74
  Personal & Witness Signatures 75

Mission Statement 76

About the Author 77

Introduction

Congratulations! You have taken the first step in planning your future and the way you are cared for in that future. By completing *"My Life, My Care, My Way,"* you will ensure that those who care for you, be it family members or complete strangers, can do so in the way you feel is appropriate for you, even if you are unable to communicate your wishes. This book will allow you to connect on a personal level, with those who will be caring for you in such a personal way.

Each of us has a very strong desire to stay as independent as possible for as long as possible. Yet very few people take advantage of the opportunity to ensure independent decision making by advance care planning. The "I'll simply cross that bridge when I come to it" way of thinking is the reason individuals do not take action. The problem is, that bridge often comes when we least expect it, leaving little if any time to plan. We plan for so many things in our lives; weddings, careers, families, retirement, travel, and financial security, yet we do not plan for our own advanced age, or for life after injury. Ask yourself this question, "If I were unable to communicate tomorrow, who would know me well enough to care for me, the way I would care for myself?" Can you answer the question with complete confidence? Since three out of five people will depend on someone else to care for them in their lifetime, the question should be, "Why not plan ahead?"

With *"My Life, My Care, My Way"* you can give your caregivers a manual on how to care for you. If you are unable to remember or communicate important details about your life, you can still share those details, in your own words. Family members, out of love, may tell caregivers how *they* would like you to be cared for, or share the interests *they* think you should participate in. Caregivers have the responsibility of caring for you as if you were their own mother or father. *"My Life, My Care, My Way"* is a window for your caregiver to see you as a person. They will be able to understand that you live an important life, with purpose and meaning. They will see that you love your family and friends and that you are loved in return. Most importantly, they will see *you*! They will see the person who wrote the book, the person they may not be able to see when they meet you.

As a Long Term Care professional for more than twenty years, I can tell you from personal experience, the better your caregivers understand and know you, the better equipped they will be to give you quality, compassionate and loving care.

This book will serve you in so many ways. It will be used as an official record of your thoughts and feelings about medical care. It can also be a keepsake for your family or close friends. This book can be used in your home, with home health care workers, or family members giving care, as well as a bedside manual for health care facilities you may reside in.

This book can also serve as an important tool in choosing a long term care facility. The current movement in long term care is "Resident Centered Care." This means the resident has complete ownership of their care. If you, or your family, are looking for a retirement community, assisted living facility or nursing home you will want to take this book with you. Ask those you communicate with in the facility how they would incorporate the use of *"My Life, My Care, My Way"*. If they do not seem open to using it, the facility may not be as interested in resident centered care as you are.

Suggestions for Completing
My Life, My Care, My Way

The first rule is, there are no rules. This is your book; use it as you see fit. The following are suggestions for completing and using the book so that it becomes the best possible tool for you and those who care for you.

- **TALK TO YOUR FAMILY!** - Make certain your family knows about this document. Have a conversation with them about your wishes and have them read it so there is no confusion about what you are requesting.

- **TALK TO YOUR DOCTOR!** - I strongly recommend initiating a conversation with your physician about the health care directives included in this book so you both have a clear understanding of what you are requesting.

- **WRITE LEGIBLY!** - You may want to print your responses to ensure your caregivers do not have difficulty reading what you have written.

- **BE HONEST!** - The only way someone can truly care for you is if they know the truth about how you wish to be cared for. Don't worry about how it sounds or what someone else might think. This is your life, your way. Be honest about how you want to live it.

- **TAKE YOUR TIME!** - This book doesn't have to be filled out the same day you get it. Think about the statements and do a few pages at a time so it doesn't become an overwhelming task.

  — By the same token, don't leave the book blank. It won't do you or a future caregiver much good if there is no information recorded.

- **COMPLETING STATEMENTS!**

  — Read through the sections before you begin filling out the pages. You may find that a statement strikes you differently after having read other statements in the section.

  — If you do not understand what information a statement is asking for, complete the statement as you understand it. Remember, there are no wrong answers in a book that you write.

  — Some statements may not apply at this time in your life, but will be useful in the future. Leave these statements blank and fill them in as they become appropriate.

  — If there are blanks that will never apply to you, write in N/A (non-applicable) or cross them out.

— If you need assistance filling out your book, ask someone you trust to help you. A close family member may really enjoy spending the time with you, getting to know you even better.

— If you need more space, have additional thoughts that are not expressed by the statements, or want to add additional names or telephone numbers feel free to do this. You can add pages or write on the back of pages anywhere you like.

— Do not feel you have to fill in all the lines on longer statements. Simply answer the statement the way you wish it to be read and you're done!

- **UPDATE YOUR INFOMATION**! - As time goes by you may find your wishes have changed. It's a good idea to look over your answers occasionally and update the information as needed.

— If you choose to update or change your responses, put a simple line through the original statement, then date and initial it. This will assure those who read this book that it was you who made the changes.

- **BE SPECIFIC**! - Remember, the more information you give someone the better care they can give you.

— If there is information you do not want your caregivers to know, do not include it. If you think it is important for them to know, include only the details they need to give you quality care.

- **SIGNITURES & DATES**! - As you complete each page, sign and date where indicated. This will give caregivers an idea of when you wrote your wishes. When the book is complete, you will want to sign and date the document in the presence of two witnesses, who will also sign and date it. You may also choose to have a notary as a witness, and/or an attorney.

Finally, have fun! This can be a time of happy memories. It will be a gift your family, friends, and caregivers will cherish for a lifetime.

Personal Information

*T*here are many things about my life that would be helpful for you, my caregiver, to know. I have included some of the basic information in this section. This information will give you insight into my personality and how and why I react in certain situations. It will also provide ideas which will help us relate to one another. I have lived an important life. The more you understand and know about me as a person, the easier your job as a caregiver will become.

Me

My full given name is _____,

but you can call me _____

I was born on _____, _____

In the town of _____, in the state of _____

In the country _____

My Family

My Mother's full name is _____

She was born on _____ in _____

She passed away on _____

She is buried _____

My Father's full name is _____

She was born on _____ in _____

He passed away on _____

He is buried _____

My Parent's children include:

_____

_____

_____

_____

_____

My Spouse's full name is _____

Who was born on _____ in _____

Our Wedding Anniversary is _____

My Spouse passed away on _____

My Spouse is buried _____

Completed By: _____ *Date:* _____

12

My Children include

_____ Born on _____
_____ Born on _____
_____ Born on _____
_____ Born on _____
_____ Born on _____
_____ Born on _____

Other important family members include

_____ Born on _____
_____ Born on _____
_____ Born on _____
_____ Born on _____

Ethnic Background

My Mother's family origins are _____

_____

_____

My Father's family origins are _____

_____

_____

Languages that I speak fluently are _____

Languages that I speak occasionally are _____

Education

I attended elementary school at _____

I attended high school at _____

I attended college at _____

And majored in _____

Completed By: _____ *Date:* _____

PERSONAL INFORMATION

I received additional education from _____

I hold degrees, certification, licensure, in _____

My favorite subjects were _____

My least favorite subjects were _____

My feelings about my education are _____

Occupations I have had include _____

My Military experience includes _____

Health Care

The **Doctor** I am comfortable with is _____

If I had to change doctors I _____

The **Clinic** I am comfortable with is _____

If I had to change clinics I _____

Completed By: _____ *Date:* _____

The **Hospital** I am comfortable with is _____

If I had to change hospitals I _____
_____

The **Dentist** I am comfortable with is _____

If I had to change dentists I _____
_____

The **Eye Doctor** I am comfortable with is _____

If I had to change eye doctors I _____
_____

Politics

When it comes to political parties, I consider myself a _____

When I vote I take into consideration _____
_____
_____

My general feelings about politics and voting _____
_____
_____

If I am able and have the choice to vote or not to vote I would choose to_____
_____

Religion & Spirituality

The religious/spiritual facility I do or have attended is _____

My religious affiliation is _____

As far as my religious and spiritual beliefs, I feel _____
_____
_____
_____

Completed By: _____ *Date:* _____

PERSONAL INFORMATION

I was raised to believe _____

_____

_____

_____

_____

_____

I have discovered for myself that _____

_____

_____

_____

The spiritual practices I would like to continue to be involved with include _____

_____

_____

_____

You can help me to do this by _____

_____

_____

_____

I am comforted by my beliefs because _____

_____

_____

_____

Spiritual people I can speak with about my feelings, values and beliefs are

_____ Telephone: _____

_____ Telephone: _____

_____ Telephone: _____

_____ Telephone: _____

Completed By: _____ *Date:* _____

Adaptive Equipment (dentures, walker, cane, glasses, hearing aids...)

The types of devices I use to assist me include _____
_____
_____

What you should know about the way in which I use these devices is _____
_____
_____
_____

Devices I am concerned about using in the future are _____
_____

The reasons I am concerned are _____
_____
_____

If I need to use these devices you can help me by _____
_____
_____
_____

How I Communicate

When spoken to, I understand more clearly if the speaker _____
_____
_____

I have challenges understanding when a speaker _____
_____
_____
_____

When I am **happy**, I show it by _____
_____

Completed By: _____ *Date:* _____

PERSONAL INFORMATION

When I am **angry**, I show it by _____
_____

When I am **sad**, I show it by _____
_____

When I am **annoyed**, I show it by _____
_____

When I am **afraid**, I show it by _____
_____

I make decisions by _____
_____
_____
_____

Challenges I have expressing my needs to others are _____
_____
_____
_____

I would describe my general personality as _____
_____
_____
_____

I believe humor in communication is _____
_____
_____
_____

When I communicate with others, I avoid_____
_____
_____
_____

Completed By: _____ *Date:* _____

My Ideal Life

When I think about myself as an older person, I believe the ideal life for me _____
_____
_____
_____
_____
_____
_____
_____
_____
_____

Thinking Ahead

If I could plan the last year of my life, _____
_____
_____
_____
_____
_____
_____
_____
_____
_____
_____

Completed By: _____ *Date:* _____

PERSONAL INFORMATION

Additional Thoughts, Photos, Clippings

Completed By: _____ *Date:* _____

COMFORTS

I would like to share my thoughts, habits, and routines which have become part of my lifestyle and give me comfort. I would ask that you look at these items and remember that I am my own person, with my own personal history. If you have challenges caring for me, you may find something in this section that will make all the difference in my comfort and in the way I accept care from you. Again, I would like to thank you for your love and compassion as you care for me.

How I Like to Present Myself

I have always been the type of person who likes to dress _____

_____

My favorite types of clothing are _____

_____

_____

Colors that I enjoy wearing are _____

_____

Colors that I do not like to wear are _____

What you would never see me wear _____

_____

I prefer fabric that _____

I like my clothes to fit _____

The weight I am comfortable at is _____ pounds.

If I lost weight I would feel _____

If I gained weight I would feel _____

My most recent sizes as of _____ include:
(DATE)

Pants: _____ Undergarments: _____
                                 (Specify Type)
Shirts: _____   _____

Shoes: _____   _____

Coat: _____ Gloves: _____

Dress: _____ Stockings/Socks: _____

My most recent sizes as of _____ include:
(DATE)

Pants: _____ Undergarments: _____
                                 (Specify Type)
Shirts: _____   _____

Shoes: _____   _____

Coat: _____ Gloves: _____

Dress: _____ Stockings/Socks: _____

Completed By: _____ *Date:* _____

My most recent sizes as of _____ include:
(DATE)

Pants: _____ Undergarments: _____
(Specify Type)
Shirts: _____ _____

Shoes: _____ _____

Coat: _____ Gloves: _____

Dress: _____ Stockings/Socks: _____

When the temperature is hot I like to wear _____

When the temperature is cool I like to wear _____

When the temperature is cold I like to wear _____

My favorite style of shoes is _____

My Personal Appearance

I like to wear my hair _____

I get my hair cut/styled (how often) _____

The person(s) I most trust to work with my hair is _____

Their telephone number is _____

The things I never want done to my hair are _____

My favorite perfume/cologne is _____

When it comes to jewelry I _____

_____

_____

Other things about my appearance you should know (makeup, fingernails, toenails, shaving)

_____

_____

_____

_____

Completed By: _____ *Date:* _____

My Daily Routine

A typical day for me looks like:

7:00am _____

8:00am _____

9:00am _____

10:00am _____

11:00am _____

12:00pm _____

1:00pm _____

2:00pm _____

3:00pm _____

4:00pm _____

5:00pm _____

6:00pm _____

7:00pm _____

8:00pm _____

9:00pm _____

10:00pm _____

11:00pm _____

Additional Time is spent _____

_____

When my routine is interrupted I tend to _____

_____

_____

Room Temperature

I like the room temperature to feel _____

When I am hot I _____

When I am cold I _____

When it rains I _____

Completed By: _____ *Date:* _____

Sleep Routine

I like to go to bed around _____ and get up about _____

I stay up later when _____

I get up earlier when _____

The things I do to get ready for bed include _____

_____

_____

_____

The sleeping position I am most comfortable in _____

_____

For pillows I like _____

For blankets I like _____

When I sleep I like to wear _____

I like my sleeping room temperature to be _____

When I sleep I always like (window open, TV on, pillow between knees), _____

_____

_____

If I am having difficulty sleeping, the problem might be _____

_____

_____

_____

Eating Habits

My routine for eating meals and snacks includes _____

_____

_____

_____

Completed By: _____ *Date:* _____

COMFORTS

I like to eat **breakfast** around _____

My favorite **breakfast** foods are _____
_____

My least favorite **breakfast** foods are _____
_____

I like to eat **lunch** around _____

My favorite **lunch** foods are _____
_____

My least favorite **lunch** foods are _____
_____

I like to eat **dinner** around _____

My favorite **dinner** foods are _____
_____

My least favorite **dinner** foods are _____
_____

I like to eat **snacks** around _____

My favorite **snacks** are_____
_____

My least favorite **snacks** are _____
_____

My favorite **beverages** are _____
_____

Foods that I will not eat are _____
_____

When it comes to the **temperature** of my food _____
_____

When it comes to the **seasoning** of my food I prefer _____
_____

Food allergies I have include _____
_____

Completed By: _____ *Date:* _____

Bathing Preferences

When it comes to bathing I prefer to take a ☐ Bath ☐ Shower

I like the **water temperature** to be _____

The **soap** I like to use is _____

The **shampoo** I like to use is _____

The **conditioner** I like to use is _____

Other **bath products** I like to use are _____

The **toothpaste** I prefer to use is _____

The **skin moisturizer** I prefer to use is _____

The **deodorant** I prefer to use is _____

I like to take a shower or bath (number of times per week) _____

If someone had to assist me with bathing I would feel _____
_____

I would prefer to have a ☐ Female ☐ Male assistant help me with bathing.

You can help me adjust to bathing with assistance by _____
_____
_____
_____

Other things you should know about my bathing preferences _____
_____

Volume Preferences

When someone speaks to me I can hear best when they speak _____
_____

I hear best in my _____ ear

If there is background noise I _____

When I watch TV, I like to set the volume _____

When I listen to the radio, I like to set the volume _____

Completed By: _____ *Date:* _____

27

Visual Preferences

I ☐ Do   ☐ Do Not   wear glasses.

I ☐ Do   ☐ Do Not   wear contact lenses.

The smallest print I am able to read is:

_____Small Print

_____Regular Size Print

_____**Headline Size Print**

_____**Large Print**

_____Unable To Make Out Print

I am able to see best when the room lighting is _____
_____

I am able to read or do activities with my hands best when the lighting is _____
_____

You can assist me to read by _____
_____

Relaxation

I feel the most tension when _____

When I want to relax, I _____

I feel the most relaxed when _____
_____

Music makes me feel _____
_____

The music I enjoy listening to, that helps me relax is _____
_____

Smells I love include _____
_____

Completed By: _____ *Date:* _____

Exercise Practices

When it comes to exercise I _____

_____

Exercises I enjoy doing include _____

_____

_____

The amount that I am comfortable exercising _____

_____

If I were asked to exercise more, by a doctor or healthcare provider, I would _____

_____

_____

_____

Objects of Comfort

My most prized possessions include _____

_____

_____

If I ever move to a care facility, the things that must accompany me are _____

_____

_____

Possessions which have fond memories for me and may bring me joy if I am unable to communicate with you include _____

_____

_____

If I moved to a healthcare facility, I am concerned about leaving behind _____

_____

_____

_____

Completed By: _____ *Date:* _____

Other Things That Give Me Comfort

_____
_____
_____
_____
_____
_____
_____
_____
_____
_____

Additional Thoughts, Photos, Clippings

_____
_____
_____
_____
_____
_____
_____
_____
_____
_____
_____
_____
_____

Completed By: _____ *Date:* _____

INTERESTS & ACTIVITIES

I would like you to know how I enjoy spending my time. Remember that I am a person with my own interests. Here you will find many ideas on how to help me continue to enjoy my life. I may not be able to do all of these activities in the usual way, but perhaps, there is a way for you to adapt the activities to my current abilities. Figuring out how to participate in these activities will be fun for both of us.

My Interests and Activities

My favorite thing to do in my spare time is _____
_____
_____
_____
_____

Some things I used to enjoy doing, but haven't done recently are _____
_____
_____

The reason I haven't done these activities _____
_____
_____

My hobbies, past and present, include _____
_____
_____
_____
_____

A typical day of activity for me includes _____
_____
_____
_____
_____

Things I enjoy doing, but don't do as often include _____
_____
_____
_____
_____
_____

Completed By: _____ *Date:* _____

Activities that I do not enjoy doing are _____

_____

_____

_____

Activity supplies that I would like to have available for me in my home or another facility include_____

_____

_____

_____

_____

_____

My Favorites

Television Programs:

Show _____ Day/Time _____ Channel _____

Show _____ Day/Time _____ Channel _____

Show _____ Day/Time _____ Channel _____

Show _____ Day/Time _____ Channel _____

Movies: _____

_____

_____

_____

Radio Stations: _____

Types of Music: _____

_____

Songs: _____

_____

Completed By: _____ *Date:* _____

INTERESTS & ACTIVITIES

Magazines: _____
_____
_____

Books: _____
_____
_____

Pets

In my opinion, pets are _____
_____

Pets I have had in my lifetime are _____
_____

If I am unable to keep my pet(s) with me, I want to make sure _____
_____
_____
_____

Animals that I do not want around me are _____

If I am in a facility that has animals, you should know _____
_____
_____
_____

If I am unable to keep my pets with me, you can best help me adjust by _____
_____
_____
_____
_____

Completed By: _____ *Date:* _____

My Accomplishments

I believe I am most talented at _____
_____
_____

My greatest accomplishments in life include _____
_____
_____
_____
_____
_____
_____

Awards I have received include _____
_____
_____
_____
_____
_____

My Social Circle

When I think about spending time alone I feel _____
_____
_____
_____

Things I enjoy doing on my own are _____
_____
_____
_____

Completed By: _____ *Date:* _____

INTERESTS & ACTIVITIES

When I think about spending time in a group I feel _____
_____
_____
_____

Things I enjoy doing in a group are _____
_____
_____

Community groups, church groups, or clubs I belong to or have belonged to include
_____
_____
_____
_____

The family member I am closest to is _____
The reason we are so close _____
_____
_____

The person, other than family, I am closest to is _____
The reason we are so close _____
_____
_____

Friends that I like to stay in contact with include (include telephone numbers)
_____ Telephone: _____
_____ Telephone: _____
_____ Telephone: _____
_____ Telephone: _____
_____ Telephone: _____
_____ Telephone: _____
_____ Telephone: _____

Completed By: _____ *Date:* _____

Activities I enjoy doing with my friends include _____

_____

_____

_____

Interests and activities I am concerned about giving up as I age include _____

_____

_____

_____

When I think about doing activities in a care facility I _____

_____

_____

_____

If I need to be in a nursing home, the way I would like the activity staff to encourage me is

_____

_____

_____

_____

Other things I would like you to know about my Interests and activities are _____

_____

_____

_____

_____

_____

_____

_____

_____

_____

Completed By: _____ *Date:* _____

INTERESTS & ACTIVITIES

My Favorite Holidays & Traditions

Completed By: _____ *Date:* _____

LIFE HISTORY

*T*he following are aspects of my life that may be very personal to me. I am telling you these things so that you will better understand how and why I react to different situations. This information may help you care for me when I am having a difficult time, or when my behavior is out of the ordinary. These thoughts about my life may also help you, help me, to recall cherished memories I am unable to remember on my own. Thank you for treating me, and my memories, with care and compassion.

My Family

My life as a child was _____

_____

_____

_____

_____

My Memories of my Mother

_____

_____

_____

_____

_____

_____

_____

_____

_____

_____

My Memories of my Father

_____

_____

_____

_____

_____

_____

_____

_____

_____

_____

Completed By: _____ *Date:* _____

photo of yourself as a child

Myself As a Child in the Year_____ at age of_____

photo of your mother

photo of your father

My Mother in the Year_____

My Father in the Year_____

Completed By: _____ *Date:* _____

LIFE HISTORY

My Memories of my Spouse

Completed By: _____ *Date:* _____

photo of your spouse

photo of your wedding day

My Spouse in the Year _____

At the Age of _____

On Our Wedding Day

_____
wedding date

Memories of My Wedding

_____
_____
_____
_____
_____
_____

Completed By: _____ *Date:* _____

LIFE HISTORY

|photo of your child|photo of your child|

This is _____   This is _____

At the age of _____   At the age of _____

|photo of your child|photo of your child|

This is _____   This is _____

At the age of _____   At the age of _____

|photo of your child|photo of your child|

This is _____   This is _____

At the age of _____   At the age of _____

Completed By: _____   *Date:* _____

My Memories of my Children

Completed By: _____ Date: _____

LIFE HISTORY

My memories of my Grandchildren

Completed By: _____ Date: _____

[photo of your grandchild] [photo of your grandchild]

This is _____ This is _____

At the age of _____ At the age of _____

[photo of your grandchild] [photo of your grandchild]

This is _____ This is _____

At the age of _____ At the age of _____

[photo of your grandchild] [photo of your grandchild]

This is _____ This is _____

At the age of _____ At the age of _____

Completed By: _____   *Date:* _____

LIFE HISTORY

My memories of my Grandparents

_____
_____
_____
_____
_____
_____
_____
_____
_____
_____
_____
_____
_____
_____

My memories of my Siblings

_____
_____
_____
_____
_____
_____
_____
_____
_____
_____
_____
_____
_____
_____
_____

Completed By: _____ *Date:* _____

Life Review

The happiest time in my life was _____

_____

_____

_____

_____

_____

_____

_____

_____

_____

_____

_____

_____

The scariest time in my life was _____

_____

_____

_____

_____

_____

_____

_____

_____

Completed By: _____ *Date:* _____

LIFE HISTORY

The saddest time in my life was _____

_____

_____

_____

_____

_____

_____

_____

If I could do one thing in my life, it would be _____

_____

_____

_____

_____

_____

_____

_____

Some significant losses in my life have included _____

_____

_____

_____

_____

_____

_____

_____

Completed By: _____ *Date:* _____

What I have learned through loss is _____
_____
_____
_____
_____
_____
_____
_____

I am happy that _____
_____
_____
_____
_____
_____
_____
_____

I am proud of _____
_____
_____
_____
_____
_____
_____
_____

Completed By: _____ *Date:* _____

LIFE HISTORY

I am afraid of _____

_____

_____

_____

_____

_____

_____

I regret _____

_____

_____

_____

_____

_____

_____

Things that make me laugh are _____

_____

_____

_____

_____

_____

_____

Completed By: _____ *Date:* _____

Time of My Life

The following memories are from each decade of my life. There may be times when I believe I am younger than I am. Should this happen you will be able to see what events were happening in my life at that time and communicate with me in a loving and compassionate manner. If I become difficult to communicate with because of memory loss or dementia, ask me my age. You can also ask the ages of my children or spouse, or any significant person in my life. This will give you a clue as to what reality I am living in. Please do not try to convince me that reality is different than I believe. This will only cause me distress. Simply step into my reality and give me peace and reassurance by allowing me the freedom to be who I am, at whatever age I am.

In my teens _____

_____

_____

_____

_____

_____

_____

_____

_____

_____

_____

_____

_____

_____

_____

_____

Completed By: _____ *Date:* _____

In my twenties _____

_____

_____

_____

_____

_____

_____

_____

_____

_____

_____

_____

_____

_____

In my thirties _____

_____

_____

_____

_____

_____

_____

_____

_____

_____

_____

_____

_____

_____

Completed By: _____ *Date:* _____

In my forties _____

In my fifties _____

Completed By: _____ Date: _____

In my sixties _____

_____

In my seventies _____

Completed By: _____ Date: _____

In my eighties _____

_____

In my nineties _____

_____

Completed By: _____ Date: _____

Life History

When I became a centenarian _____

_____
_____
_____
_____
_____
_____
_____
_____
_____
_____
_____
_____
_____
_____
_____

Additional Thoughts, Photos, Clippings

_____
_____
_____
_____
_____
_____
_____
_____
_____
_____
_____

Completed By: _____ *Date:* _____

PERSONAL DIRECTIVES

Should I become incapacitated and unable to manage medical and legal situations, I want anyone who cares about me, and for me, to know in my own words, the details of my personal care that are important to me.

Legal Matters

The person(s) to contact with legal questions is _____

The phone number is _____

Legal documents that I have completed are _____

_____

_____

_____

_____

If you have questions about these documents (such as where to find them, are they completed, or if they are requested by a doctor or care facility), you may contact the person(s) listed above.

Legal documents I have chosen to keep in this book are _____

_____

_____

_____

If you do not find these documents in this book please contact the person(s) listed above.

Financial Matters

The person(s) to contact with financial questions is _____

The phone number is _____

Financial documents that I have completed are _____

_____

_____

_____

_____

If you have questions about these documents (such as where to find them, are they completed, or if they are requested by a doctor or care facility), you may contact the person(s) listed above.

Completed By: _____ *Date:* _____

Financial documents I have chosen to keep in this book are _____

_____

_____

_____

_____

If you do not find these documents in this book, please contact the person(s) listed on the previous page.

Legal Healthcare Directives

The person(s) I trust to make or help me make healthcare decisions is/are _____

_____

The phone number is _____

I, _____, ☐ Do ☐ Do Not have a living will and/or advance directives completed and on record with an attorney or medical doctor.

This document can be found _____

My Thoughts on Home Health Care

What I have come to believe about home health care is _____

_____

_____

_____

_____

If I needed to have home health care I would feel _____

_____

_____

_____

The challenges I see myself having with home health care are _____

_____

_____

Completed By: _____ *Date:* _____

What will help ease those challenges _____

_____

_____

_____

_____

Home Health services I would be willing to accept are:

☐ Cleaning ☐ Cooking ☐ Grooming ☐ Personal Care

☐ Financial ☐ Companionship ☐ Physical/Occupational/Speech Therapy

☐ Emergency Response Monitor/Necklace ☐ Legal Assistance ☐ Transportation

My Thoughts on Assisted Living

What I have come to believe about assisted living is _____

_____

_____

_____

_____

If I needed to be in an assisted living facility I would feel _____

_____

_____

_____

_____

_____

The challenges I see myself having in an assisted living facility are _____

_____

_____

_____

_____

_____

Completed By: _____ *Date:* _____

What will help ease those challenges _____
_____
_____
_____
_____

The assisted living facilities I would prefer to live in, if need be, are in order of preference.

1. _____
2. _____
3. _____

My Thoughts on Nursing Home Care

What I have come to believe about nursing homes is _____
_____
_____
_____
_____

If I needed to live in a nursing home I would feel _____
_____
_____
_____
_____

You can best help me to adapt to life in a nursing home by _____
_____
_____
_____
_____

Completed By: _____ *Date:* _____

The challenges I see myself having in a nursing home are _____

_____
_____
_____
_____

What will help ease those challenges _____

_____
_____
_____
_____

The nursing homes I would prefer to live in, if need be, are in order by preference.

    1. _____

    2. _____

    3. _____

If I need to have a roommate, some things to take into consideration _____

_____
_____
_____
_____

Completed By: _____ *Date:* _____

Medical Care

I would prefer to be cared for by ☐ Female ☐ Male assistants.

If my caregivers feel I need to use mobility devices, such as a walker or wheelchair, I would like to have the freedom to _____

_____

_____

_____

_____

The amount of risk I am willing to take to have this freedom _____

_____

_____

_____

_____

My thoughts on physical restraints being used while I'm in a health care facility (bedrails, wheelchair restraints, medications) _____

_____

_____

_____

_____

When it comes to pain tolerance I _____

_____

_____

_____

_____

Completed By: _____ *Date:* _____

I feel **pain medications** should be used when _____

_____

_____

_____

_____

But not used when _____

_____

_____

_____

_____

I feel a **hydration and/or feeding tube** to sustain my life should be used when _____

_____

_____

_____

_____

But not used when _____

_____

_____

_____

_____

I feel **CPR**, to resuscitate my heart, should be used when _____

_____

_____

_____

_____

Completed By: _____ *Date:* _____

But not used when _____

_____

_____

_____

_____

My thoughts on **withholding water and nourishment** _____

_____

_____

_____

_____

The circumstances under which this would be **appropriate** for me _____

_____

_____

_____

_____

The circumstances under which this would be **inappropriate** for me _____

_____

_____

_____

_____

In the event my food needs to be altered (thickened, pureed, thinned) in order to continue to eat or drink I feel _____

_____

_____

_____

Completed By: _____ *Date:* _____

Risks I am willing to take, when it comes to eating and drinking include _____

_____

_____

_____

_____

Care For My Pet

If I am unable to care for my pet my wishes are _____

_____

_____

_____

_____

My pet's veterinarian is _____

The telephone number is _____

The kennel where I take my pet is _____

The telephone number is _____

The person I trust to make decisions about my pet if I am unable to is:

_____

The telephone number is _____

Spiritual Care

My thoughts on spiritual care are _____

_____

_____

_____

_____

Spiritual leaders I would like to continue contact with include _____

_____

Completed By: _____ *Date:* _____

The telephone numbers are _____

The extent to which I would like to continue to be spiritually involved _____
_____
_____
_____
_____

End of Life Care

When I think about the end of my life I _____
_____
_____
_____
_____
_____
_____
_____
_____
_____

My thoughts on hospice care are _____
_____
_____
_____

In the event my death is eminent, I would like to receive care that _____
_____
_____
_____
_____

Completed By: _____ *Date:* _____

PERSONAL DIRECTIVES

The people I would like to have with me, at the end of my life are

_____ Telephone number _____

_____ Telephone number _____

_____ Telephone number _____

_____ Telephone number _____

The spiritual leader to contact when my death is eminent is _____
_____

The telephone number is _____

I feel comfort care at the end of my life should include _____
_____
_____
_____
_____
_____
_____
_____

At the end of my life, I would like the environment around me to be _____
_____
_____
_____
_____

At the end of my life, the most important thing for you to know _____
_____
_____
_____
_____
_____
_____

Completed By: _____ *Date:* _____

Upon My Death

In the event of my death the people that need to be contacted immediately are

_____Telephone number _____

_____Telephone number _____

_____Telephone number _____

_____Telephone number _____

_____Telephone number _____

The mortuary to contact upon my death is _____

The telephone number is _____

The spiritual leader to contact upon my death is

_____

The telephone number is _____

My thoughts on organ donation and the plans I have made _____

_____

_____

_____

☐ I prefer a **Cemetery Burial**   At_____Cemetary

My wish for the viewing is that the casket be ☐ Open   ☐ Closed

_____

_____

_____

_____

☐ I prefer **Cremation**   I would like my ashes to be_____

_____

_____

_____

_____

Completed By: _____   *Date:* _____

My Funeral

Prior arrangements that have been made include _____

_____

_____

_____

_____

The location I would like my service to be held is _____

_____

The contact person is _____

The telephone number is _____

I would like the service to be   ☐ Open to the public   ☐ Private (Family only)

The clergy, or person, I wish to preside over my service is _____

_____

The telephone number is _____

I would like the following people to speak at the service

_____Telephone number _____

_____Telephone number _____

_____Telephone number _____

The scripture and/or readings I would like read include _____

_____

_____

_____

_____

_____

Completed By: _____   *Date:* _____

The music selections I would like include

Selection _____ **Composer** _____

Performer _____ Telephone number _____

Selection _____ **Composer** _____

Performer _____ Telephone number _____

Selection _____ **Composer** _____

Performer _____ Telephone number _____

Selection _____ **Composer** _____

Performer _____ Telephone number _____

I would like the following people to act as **pallbearers**

_____ Telephone number _____

_____ Telephone number _____

_____ Telephone number _____

_____ Telephone number _____

_____ Telephone number _____

_____ Telephone number _____

_____ Telephone number _____

_____ Telephone number _____

Special Requests

_____

_____

_____

_____

_____

_____

Completed By: _____ *Date:* _____

PERSONAL DIRECTIVES

A Personal Letter to My Family

Completed By: _____ *Date:* _____

In Conclusion

I would like to thank you for the time you have taken to read my wishes. I hope that by seeing my thoughts on paper, you have been able to see me as the real, true, authentic person that I am and always have been. I look forward to living the life I have become accustomed to, with you to assist me. Thank you again. You truly are a giver of care.

Sincerely, _____

Date of completion _____

Witness Signature _____

Date: _____

Witness Signature _____

Date: _____

Mission Statement

The mission of Bold Transitions is to empower older adults to live bold, creative, and dignified lives through the products we create, the training we provide, and by dynamic speaking and consulting, either directly with, or through those that assist in their care.

About the Author

photo by Roger LePage

Personalized, compassionate, and quality long-term healthcare is the passion on which **Paula Harder Kenemore** has built her career for more then twenty years. Paula brings personal experience, as well as insightful and educated knowledge to her writing, speaking, and consulting work.

Paula received a B.S. degree in Speech Communication from Minnesota State University, Winona and the University of Wisconsin, Superior. She is currently pursuing a master's degree in Gerontology at Bethel University in Minneapolis. She holds her Certification in Activity Consulting from the National Certification Council for Activity Professionals. Paula has also received professional training in "Culture Change" philosophy for long-term care facilities.

Paula's career began at the age of sixteen when she began work as a nursing assistant. She has held the positions of Activity Director & Consultant and Spiritual Care & Volunteer Coordinator for facilities in the two largest nursing home corporations in the country. Paula has also provided services as an independent Dementia Care Specialist for the Minnesota-North Dakota Northern Regional Chapter of the Alzheimer's Association.

With a strong desire to improve long-term healthcare for older adults, Paula has developed workshops and trainings for healthcare professionals and is the creator of many unique programs designed for nursing home residents and their families.

Paula is the founder and C.E.O. of B.O.L.D. Transitions whose mission is to Build Older Lifestyles with Dignity. Paula is committed to improving the care we give our older population through educational workshops for family and clients, staff training and consulting, and speaking events focused on aging issues.

Paula created *"My Life, My Care, My Way"* to give healthcare decision-making back to the person it belongs to…YOU! When not at work in the healthcare industry Paula enjoys spending time with her husband Tom and their three children, Nick, Cassie, & Alex.

If you are interested in having Paula consult or speak with your group, business or organization, please call B.O.L.D. Transitions at (218) 485-4252 and visit her website at www.paulaharderkenemore.com or www.bold-transitions.com. You may also reach us at our mailing address: PO Box 452, Moose Lake, MN 55767

Lake Effect
Media

Feedback Form
B.O.L.D. Transitions

You've taken the step to plan your future and how you are cared for in that future. Now you can help others who will be taking that same step. We would love to hear your thoughts on the book. Tell us what you liked, what you didn't like, or additional information that you would like to see in this book. Take a moment to fill out this feedback form and return it by:

Mail: PO Box 452, Moose Lake, 55767   Fax: 218-485-4842
Online Feedback form: www.bold-transitions.com   Email: paula@bold-transitions.com.

NAME: _____

ADDRESS: _____
_____

CITY: _____ STATE: _____ ZIP: _____
PHONE: _____ EMAIL: _____

SIGN ME UP FOR YOUR ONLINE NEWSLETTER   ☐ Yes   ☐ No
PLEASE SEND ME MORE INFORMATION ON ☐ Speaking   ☐ Consulting
HOW DID YOU HEAR ABOUT THIS BOOK?: _____
_____

HAVE YOU CONSULTED WITH A PHYSICIAN OR LAWYER REGARDING YOUR WISHES?
☐ Yes   ☐ No

DID YOU FIND THIS BOOK HELPFUL?   (VERY) 5 4 3 2 1 (NOT AT ALL)

RATE THIS BOOK ON A SCALE OF 1-10 (POOR) 1 2 3 4 5 6 7 8 9 10 (GREAT)

IF THIS BOOK IS NOT A 10, WHAT WOULD IT TAKE, IN YOUR OPINION, TO MAKE IT A 10?
_____
_____
_____

WAS IT EASY TO USE?   (EASY) 5 4 3 2 1 (DIFFICULT)

PLEASE SHARE HOW YOU HAVE USED THE BOOK AS A WAY TO ENCOURAGE OTHERS WHO WILL USE IT (include additional page if necessary).
_____
_____
_____

NAME: _____ TITLE _____
ORGANIZATION _____
MAY WE USE YOUR COMMENTS IN OUR PROMOTIONS?   ☐ Yes   ☐ No

SIGNED: _____

☐ **Send me my FREE Audio CD Bonus** – "*Your Life, Your Care, Your Way*" by Paula Harder Kenemore, your audio companion to the book "*My Life, My Care, My Way*", for only $6.95 shipping and handling.

My Life, My Care, My Way Order Form

My Life, My Care, My Way makes a great gift for your associates, employees, friends and family members. The book can also be used as a benefit or incentive for organizations to give to their clients and customers. Customization is available on larger orders, just call or email us for details. For faster service, visit our website, call us, or fax in this order form. Thank you for your order!

NAME: _____

ORGANIZATION: _____

ADDRESS: _____

CITY: _____ STATE: _____ ZIP: _____

PHONE: _____ EMAIL: _____

Quantity Pricing:

# of copies	price per copy
1 – 4	$14.95
5 – 24	$12.95
25 – 99	$10.95
100 – 499	$9.95
500 – 999	$8.95

1000 + Call for a custom quote

PLEASE SIGN ME UP FOR YOUR EMAIL NEWSLETTER
☐ yes ☐ no

Please send me more information on:
☐ Speaking ☐ Consulting

SHIPPING: $5 FOR FIRST BOOK, ADD $1 FOR EACH ADDITIONAL BOOK. ORDERS OF 25 OR MORE, CALL FOR SHIPPING QUOTE.

SALES TAX: MINNESOTA RESIDENTS, INCLUDE 6.5% SALES TAX ON TOTAL PRICE.

ORDER QUANTITY	PRICE PER COPY	SHIPPING	TOTAL
_____	$ _____	$ _____	$ _____

METHOD OF PAYMENT

ACCOUNT NUMBER: _____ 3-digit V-code _____

☐ **CHECK** (payable to Lake Effect Media)   EXPIRATION DATE: _____

☐ VISA

☐ MASTERCARD   SIGNATURE: _____

☐ DISCOVER

☐ AMERICAN EXPRESS

MAIL TO: Lake Effect Media, P.O. Box 452, Moose Lake, MN 55767
WEBSITE: www.lakeeffectmedia.net
PHONE: 218-485-4252 • FAX: 218-485-4842
EMAIL: orders@lakeeffectmedia.net

Lake Effect Media